Original title:
Aurora's Wings

Copyright © 2024 Swan Charm
All rights reserved.

Author: Kätriin Kaldaru
ISBN HARDBACK: 978-9908-52-635-5
ISBN PAPERBACK: 978-9908-52-636-2
ISBN EBOOK: 978-9908-52-637-9

Illuminated Paths

Banners flutter in the breeze,
Laughter echoes through the trees.
Lanterns glow, a warm embrace,
Joyful hearts in this bright place.

Music dances in the air,
Every smile a vibrant glare.
Stars above like candles shine,
In this moment, all is fine.

Spirit of the Sunrise

Golden rays begin to peek,
Waking dreams as shadows leak.
Birds are singing sweet and clear,
Nature's chorus, drawing near.

Colors splash across the sky,
A new day where hopes can fly.
In the warmth of dawn's embrace,
Life awakens, full of grace.

Feathered Whispers

Softly gliding through the trees,
Whispers carried on the breeze.
Colors bright against the green,
   Nature's art, a vivid scene.

Wings adorned in playful hues,
Dancing lightly, singing tunes.
  In the stillness, joy ignites,
Echoed laughter, vibrant sights.

Dreamscapes of Light

In the twilight, magic swirls,
Dancing through the night it twirls.
Fireflies wink in secret glee,
Drifting dreams, wild and free.

Moonbeams weave a silver thread,
A tapestry in dreams we tread.
In these realms where visions blend,
Every heartbeat dares to mend.

The Colors of Infinity

Colors dance on the canvas wide,
Laughter echoes, hearts open wide.
Bubbles float with a joyful cheer,
In this moment, we hold dear.

Flickering lights in the evening glow,
Wine in hand, let the stories flow.
Friends gather close, spirits ignite,
Under the stars, a magical night.

Soaring Through the First Light

Sunrise kisses the sleeping trees,
Awakening whispers in the breeze.
Joyous flutters of wings in flight,
Chasing shadows away from sight.

Golden rays weave through the dew,
Painting the world in vibrant hue.
Laughter rings as the day begins,
Celebration dances on happy skins.

A Tapestry of Celestial Hues

Stars twinkle like diamonds bright,
Pulsing rhythms under moonlight.
Celebrations waltz with the night,
In every spark, pure delight.

A tapestry woven, dreams unfold,
Stories of adventures yet to be told.
Hearts entwined in this luster glow,
Unified in the cosmic flow.

Journey of the Glowing Skies

Banners wave in the summer air,
Children giggle without a care.
Fireworks burst with a radiant boom,
Lighting up the evening gloom.

As we journey through the vibrant night,
Every smile adds to the light.
Together we laugh, together we sing,
A harmonious dance, joy is our king.

Palettes of the Rising Sun

Colors burst across the sky,
A symphony of light and cheer,
Laughter dances in the air,
As day awakens, bright and clear.

Joyous hearts gather around,
Friendship woven, hand in hand,
Music plays, a joyful sound,
In this festive, vibrant land.

Balloons rise, a playful song,
Each shade tells a tale of love,
The rising sun, a canvas wide,
As laughter spirals high above.

In this moment, time stands still,
With every smile, the world ignites,
Palettes bright, dreams brightly birthed,
In the glow of glorious heights.

Ethereal Flight of Dreams

Stars ignite the velvet night,
Whispers carry, soft as dew,
Dancing shadows, hearts alight,
In dreams, we soar, the morning new.

A tapestry of wishes spun,
Moonlit trails on silken air,
United spirits, laughter runs,
In this festival, none compare.

Gleaming trails in twilight's glow,
Moments cherished, bright and free,
Ethereal whispers, love to show,
In each glance, the world we see.

As dawn creeps in with gentle grace,
We spread our wings, take flight once more,
In dreams alive, we find our place,
Together, forever, we explore.

Beneath the Luminous Canopy

Treetops sway with gentle grace,
Lanterns glow like fireflies,
Underneath this leafy space,
We share laughter, light, and sighs.

With every step on vibrant ground,
Footprints weave a joyful dance,
In the silence, love is found,
As we twirl in sweet romance.

Every branch holds tales untold,
In whispers soft, the stories bloom,
Beneath this canopy of gold,
Our hearts beat, dispelling gloom.

As twilight kisses the dark night,
Celebrate the warmth we find,
Beneath the stars, our spirits bright,
Together, forever, intertwined.

Wings of the Celestial Dawn

The sky blushes, a soft embrace,
With wings unfurling, dreams take flight,
Golden hues set a radiant pace,
In the dawn's glow, pure delight.

Each heartbeat matches nature's tune,
Joy radiates, a sweet refrain,
Underneath the watchful moon,
We rise together—no more pain.

Candles flicker, flames of cheer,
Whispers echo through the trees,
With every moment, we revere,
The love that dances on the breeze.

The world awakens, colors blend,
With wings adorned in morning light,
In this festive joy, we transcend,
Together, we embrace the night.

Sunlit Diplomacy of Dawn

Golden rays stretch wide,
Whispers of peace collide.
In the embrace of bright light,
Hearts unite, spirits take flight.

Colors dance on the trees,
Softly swaying with the breeze.
Morning laughter fills the air,
Joy and love everywhere.

Birds sing their sweet refrain,
Life flourishes, free from pain.
Moments shared under the sun,
In this harmony, we are one.

The Art of Soaring Skies

Balloons rise in azure dreams,
Whirling with delight it seems.
Children's laughter fills the day,
In vibrant hues, we laugh and play.

Kites dance high on gentle strings,
Celebrating all the joy it brings.
Clouds like cotton candy float,
Every heart a joyful note.

Picnics spread on grassy green,
Together we're a lively scene.
With every toast and cheerful cheer,
We weave our memories year to year.

Reflections of Radiant Dawn

Mirrored lakes in morning's glow,
Reflect the joy that we all know.
Sun-kissed paths invite our feet,
In this place where moments meet.

Laughter echoes in the air,
Friends together, without a care.
Colors swirl in vibrant dance,
Each heartbeat sings a merry chance.

Mornings draped in golden hues,
Embrace the gift of fresh new views.
As daylight breaks, we simply smile,
And cherish life's sweet, festive style.

The Lure of Morning's Palette

Painted skies awake the dawn,
Brush strokes of hope, dreams reborn.
With every hue, the world ignites,
As morning brings its warm delights.

Candles flicker, soft and bright,
Filling hearts with pure delight.
Songs of cheer rise in the air,
Creating magic everywhere.

Each sip of coffee, fragrant, rich,
In our spirits, hope we stitch.
Together in this vibrant light,
We celebrate from morn till night.

Shimmers of a New Dawn

The sky blushes with golden hues,
A gentle whisper dances in the breeze.
Joyful laughter flutters like birds,
As daybreak sings sweet melodies.

Children's giggles ripple through fields,
While petals unfold in morning's embrace.
Every shadow fades into light,
And time slows down in this sacred space.

Colors swirl, a vibrant parade,
Each heartbeat syncs with nature's song.
Fingers reach for the warm sunlight,
In the arms of hope, we all belong.

With every dawn, a promise is made,
To cherish, celebrate this perfect day.
Together we rise, hand in hand,
In this festivity, we find our way.

Colors Unleashed at Sunrise

Crimson streaks break the morning grey,
Splashing joy across the open sky.
Birds awaken, their songs ignite,
As blooms blush bright and spirits fly.

Golden rays stretch across the land,
Painting dreams with a brush of light.
Every corner feels alive today,
In the warmth, we find pure delight.

The world is draped in a festive cheer,
Where laughter dances on dewdrops clear.
Each heartbeat echoes the vibrant call,
In this symphony, love conquers all.

United, we gather, hearts aglow,
To celebrate this brilliant show.
With every breath, we share the thrill,
As colors unleashed continue to spill.

Serene Soar of Morning Glory

Gentle whispers ride the morning air,
Each petal unfolds in warm sunlight.
The world awakens with tender care,
As day spreads its wings, taking flight.

A river of silver shines and flows,
Reflecting joy from the skies above.
Harmony blooms where the soft wind blows,
In the embrace of warmth, we find love.

Together we rise with hope in our hearts,
Each moment a gift, a treasure so rare.
In fields of gold, where laughter departs,
We soar on dreams, as light fills the air.

Filling the world with warmth and grace,
In this serene morning, we find our pace.
With every sunrise, we vow and say,
Together in spirit, come what may.

Whirlwinds of Awakening Light

A rush of joy sweeps across the land,
As sunbeams twine in a playful dance.
Nature ignites with a vibrant band,
In this whirl of color, we find our chance.

The whispers of dawn coax the flowers,
To awaken from slumber, embrace the day.
In every shadow, the light empowers,
A symphony of life leads us away.

With every breeze, fresh stories unfold,
Echoing laughter, weaving time anew.
In the festive realm, where dreams are bold,
We gather together, hearts ever true.

Bathed in the glow of a waking sun,
We celebrate life, its battles won.
In the whirlwinds of joy, we unite,
Awakening light, our spirits take flight.

Chasing the Light of Early Hours

The dawn breaks bright, a golden hue,
Laughter spills like morning dew.
Colors dance upon the trees,
Whispers carried by a gentle breeze.

Joyous tunes fill the waking day,
Children's smiles in bright array.
Sunshine winks from skies so blue,
A world reborn, refreshed and new.

Festive hearts in every place,
Warmth and light, a sweet embrace.
Chasing dreams where spirits soar,
Together we laugh, together we roar.

With every step, the music sways,
We celebrate in countless ways.
As time flows on, we hold it tight,
Chasing the light, from morning to night.

Whirls of Celestial Dreams

Stars twinkle like a festive glow,
Dancing lights put on a show.
Moonbeams play on silver streams,
Igniting all our hopeful dreams.

Whirls of wishes in the night,
Each heart glimmers, pure delight.
Constellations spin and twine,
In this dance, you are truly mine.

Echoes of laughter fill the air,
Magic woven everywhere.
Our spirits lift with every sound,
In this realm, enchantment found.

Celebration hugs the starlit sky,
Underneath, we laugh and sigh.
With celestial wonders to pursue,
In whirls of dreams, I'm lost in you.

Wings of the Morning Mirage

Morning light begins to play,
Birds take flight, brightening the day.
With every flutter, sparks ignite,
A mirage of joy, a pure delight.

Fields awaken in colors so grand,
Nature's canvas, hand in hand.
Wings of promise in the breeze,
Swaying gently through the trees.

Festivity blooms in the radiant sky,
As laughter echoes, flying high.
Together we embrace the rise,
Hearts aglow with sweet surprise.

So let us soar on wings so free,
In the embrace of jubilee.
With every heartbeat, magic unfolds,
In morning's arms, our joy beholds.

The Evocative Skies

Clouds of cotton, soft and white,
Paint reflections of pure delight.
Waves of color, a painter's dream,
Under the sun's enchanting beam.

Each sunset brings a festive cheer,
As fiery hues draw us near.
We gather 'neath the vast expanse,
In awe of nature's grand romance.

The stars emerge, a glittering show,
Guiding our hearts where magic flows.
In every twinkle, stories unfold,
Whispers of wonders waiting to be told.

Under these evocative skies,
We find the spark that never dies.
With every dawn, let joy arise,
In love, in laughter—our perfect ties.

Skyward Bound in Daylight

In fields of gold, the laughter flows,
As sunlight dances, joyfully glows.
Bright blooms awaken, colors unite,
Under the sky, everything feels right.

Children play, their voices ring,
Fluttering kites, on cheerful wings.
A symphony of joy fills the air,
With every heartbeat, the world's a fair.

Whispers of breezes, sweetly they sway,
Nature's embrace marks a perfect day.
Joyful hearts, we gather around,
Together we rise, we're skyward bound.

Glimpses of the Vibrant Awakening

Morning beams spill over the hills,
Colors burst forth, excitement thrills.
With every sunrise, hope finds its way,
In the soft glow of this glorious day.

Floral scents mingle, fragrant delight,
Petals unfurl, a dazzling sight.
Birds sing sweetly, their melodies clear,
Nature's chorus, a song we hold dear.

Dancing shadows play, all around,
As joyous laughter fills the ground.
With friends beside, in light we bask,
Vibrant awakenings—our hearts unmask.

Every moment a treasure to keep,
In this celebration, our spirits leap.
Glimpses of magic, in every glance,
Unleashing the beauty of life's grand dance.

Threads of Ethereal Bliss

Gossamer threads weave through the air,
Laughter and music, a tapestry fair.
Golden sunbeams knit joy's embrace,
In every corner, a smiling face.

Whirlwinds of color, a playful parade,
Sparkling moments that never fade.
With hearts entwined and spirits so light,
We gather together in pure delight.

Bubbles of joy rise high in the sky,
Carried on breezes, they flutter and fly.
With every embrace, more love we find,
As threads of bliss, through time, unwind.

Songs of the heart, in harmony swell,
In each joyful laugh, stories to tell.
Ethereal bliss, a radiant hue,
With every gathering, our dreams come true.

Awakening of the Celestial Realm

Stars twinkle bright in evening's embrace,
Whispers of galaxies, filling the space.
In twilight's glow, dreams begin to rise,
Awakening wonders beneath starlit skies.

Comets glide swiftly, a celestial dance,
Inviting our hearts to join in the chance.
Mysteries wrapped in the night's gentle shroud,
We gather together, our spirits unbowed.

With moonlight guiding, adventures await,
Stories of stardust and love's golden fate.
The cosmos rejoices, united we stand,
Awakening dreams, hand in hand.

Every heartbeat pulses with light from afar,
In this celestial realm, we know who we are.
Together we shine, under skies so grand,
Awakening the magic, forever we'll stand.

The Awakening Canvas

Brush strokes of laughter dance in the air, Colorful dreams weave without a care. Joy spills like paint on the canvas wide, Each hue a promise, a heartfelt guide.

Balloons rise high, kissing the blue, Voices of children, bright as the dew. Smiles blossom like flowers in spring, A tapestry woven with love's sweet string.

Candles flicker, casting warm light, Echoes of music fill up the night. The world spins gently, a carousel bright, Together we bask in the festive delight.

Nature joins in with a glorious show, Banners of joy in the soft evening glow. Hearts intertwine in this magical trance, We celebrate life in a jubilant dance.

Skies Aglow

Twinkling stars in the velvet dome, Whispering dreams of a world we call home. Laughter ignites like fireworks bright, Casting spells of joy in the calm of the night.

Parades of colors, the night takes flight, Spirits uplifted, hearts pure and light. Flutes sing sweetly under the moon, Inviting the world to join in the tune.

Dancing shadows under the glow, Magic spins quietly, ebb and flow. Each heartbeat echoes the rhythm of cheer, As friendships blossom when loved ones are near.

Savoring moments that shimmer with grace, In the vastness of joy, we find our place. Together we soar, like stars in a row, Bound by the warmth of these skies aglow.

Wings of the First Light

Morning breaks gently with whispers of gold, Stories of wonder and magic unfold. The horizon ignites, a fiery embrace, Welcoming dreams in this sacred space.

Birds take to wing with jubilant cheer, Their songs a reminder that spring is here. A dance of the leaves in the soft, gentle breeze, Nature awakes in a symphony with ease.

Each day is a canvas, bright colors spread, With every new dawn, endless paths ahead. We gather in circles, our hearts intertwine, This spirited moment, a treasure divine.

Celebrate life with the sun's golden rays, In the arms of the morning, we find our ways. Let laughter ring out, let the world burst in flight, As we spread our own wings to the first light.

Shedding the Night

The curtain of twilight begins to unfurl, Stars wink in laughter as dreams start to twirl. Echoes of night gently fade into morn, As a vibrant new day greets us reborn.

Fireflies flutter, a dance on the dew, Each flicker a wish, all sparkling and true. Banners of sunlight in colors so bright, Illuminate our path, shedding the night.

Gathered together, we lift up our voice, In the heart of the moment, we all rejoice. Sweet scents of feasts fill the morning air, For love and connection, we all lay bare.

As dawn unfolds its glorious delight, We chase away shadows, welcome the light. In harmony's embrace, let us unite, Shedding the night for a future so bright.

Whispers of the Morning Light

Sunrise paints the world in gold,
Laughter dances, stories told.
Gentle breezes, soft and sweet,
Joy and hope in every beat.

Flowers bloom with colors bright,
Waking dreams from peaceful night.
Children's giggles in the air,
Love and warmth are everywhere.

Birds are singing, skies are blue,
Every heart feels something new.
Mirthful songs of life begin,
A brand new day is drawing in.

In this glow, we find our place,
Embrace the light, a warm embrace.
Whispers carry on the breeze,
In the morning, hearts at ease.

Embrace of the Dawn Breeze

Morning breaks with softest light,
Shadows fade, the world feels right.
Petals stretch to greet the day,
Hopes arise in sweet array.

Laughter mingles with the air,
At the dawn, we shed our care.
Golden rays on laughter's face,
Every moment, a warm embrace.

Songs of joy in colors blend,
With each heartbeat, hearts ascend.
Whispers echo through the trees,
In the light, we're free to tease.

Lively stories come alive,
In the morn, we all arrive.
Hand in hand, our spirits soar,
In the dawn, we want for more.

Radiant Horizons Unfurled

Sunlit trails and skies so clear,
Gather 'round, the time is near.
Dreams take flight on wings of hope,
In the light, we learn to cope.

Hearts are racing, laughter loud,
Swaying gently with the crowd.
Colors burst in joyous cheer,
Radiance shines while we draw near.

Festive spirits in the air,
Every glance, a moment rare.
With each twirl, our worries fade,
In the dance, our fears are laid.

As the sun paints gold and pink,
We join voices, hearts in sync.
Horizons stretch, and dreams unfold,
In our stories, joy is told.

Symphony of the Awakening Sky

Chiming bells and voices bright,
Echo through the morning light.
Every petal, leaf and tree,
Sings a tune so wild and free.

Luminous dawns invite us near,
Hearts ablaze with festive cheer.
Colors twirl in playful dance,
In this moment, take a chance.

Whispers of the day ahead,
Life awakens, dreams are fed.
Notes of laughter fill the air,
In this symphony, we share.

Joyful echoes touch the heart,
In this world, we're each a part.
Embrace the light, the song, the play,
In these moments, forever stay.

Heartbeats of the Awakening Sky

In the morning glow, laughter wakes,
Colors dance as the sunlight breaks.
Joyful whispers breeze through the trees,
Nature sings with the buzzing bees.

Clouds adorned in splashes bright,
Birds take flight in pure delight.
Every heartbeat syncs with the dawn,
Celebration springs as night is gone.

Fields alive with vibrant blooms,
Echoes of joy in sunlit rooms.
The world awakens, spirits soar,
Together we dance, forevermore.

Hands held high, we greet the day,
With each heartbeat, we find our way.
In the sky's embrace, we ignite,
A festival of love, pure and bright.

The Flight of Daybreak Dreams

Awakening whispers in the air,
Dancing shadows swirl everywhere.
The rosy hues gently appear,
Dreams take flight, banishing fear.

Soft golden rays kiss the ground,
Joy awakens in the sound.
With every step, hope comes alive,
A vibrant spark that helps us thrive.

Mirthful laughter fills the park,
Children playing until it's dark.
Kites soar high in the azure sky,
With each cheer, our spirits fly.

The heart of daybreak beats so strong,
In this celebration, we belong.
Together we dream, together we play,
In the magic of dawn's bright ballet.

Kaleidoscope of Dawn's Embrace

Colors swirl in morning's light,
A kaleidoscope, pure delight.
Nature's brush in joyful strokes,
Dancing dreams in vibrant folks.

Sunrise paints the world anew,
Each shade whispers tales so true.
The breeze carries laughter's sound,
In this magic, joy is found.

Hope ignites in every glance,
Hearts entwined in a merry dance.
Flowers bloom, horizons wide,
With every heartbeat, we abide.

Together we weave this tapestry,
In every thread, our legacy.
Dawn's embrace wraps us tight,
In this festival of pure insight.

Harmonies of Luminous Echoes

Evening fades, stars start to gleam,
Echoing the whispers of a dream.
In the twilight, an orchestra plays,
Melodies weave through the soft haze.

Candles flicker, their flames a glow,
Guiding us where the feelings flow.
Voices rising, hand in hand,
In this moment, we all stand.

Moonlit paths shimmer and shine,
Hearts connect, forever entwined.
A symphony sings in the night,
With every note, we take flight.

Harmony fills the vibrant air,
In this festivity, beyond compare.
Together, we share this mystical dance,
In luminous echoes, we find our chance.

The Rapture of Renewal

Balloons rise bright, a joyous sight,
Confetti dances in the soft sunlight.
Laughter echoes, hearts set free,
We celebrate life, just you and me.

Fresh blooms burst in vibrant hues,
Chasing away the winter blues.
Each moment sparkles, pure delight,
As we embrace this festive night.

Songs of happiness fill the air,
With friends around, there's love to share.
Golden moments we hold tight,
In the rapture, all feels right.

Together we create, renew the flame,
In every whisper, we're never the same.
Tomorrow beckons with open hands,
In the rapture, united we stand.

Celestial Horizons

Stars ignite in velvet skies,
As laughter blooms and spirits rise.
A tapestry of dreams unfolds,
In every heart, a story told.

Dancing shadows twirl and glide,
In this moment, nothing hides.
Each twinkle matches a joyful cheer,
Echoing warmth as loved ones near.

The moon bestows its silver light,
Guiding our souls through the night.
Hands entwined, we sway and sing,
To the joy that this night can bring.

With every heartbeat, every glance,
We weave together in a dance.
In celestial mirrors, we find our place,
Festive spirits in an endless embrace.

Whispers of the Dawn

Bright hues gather with the morning glow,
As whispers of joy begin to flow.
The sun spills gold on dew-kissed grass,
In this new day, our worries pass.

Birds awaken, their songs align,
Each note a wish, each chirp divine.
Together we rise, embrace the light,
In whispers of dawn, hearts take flight.

A fragrant breeze carries laughter's tune,
Painting the day beneath the moon.
With every sunrise, hope is reborn,
In this festival, we greet the morn.

Layered moments, precious and sweet,
Together we dance, our spirits meet.
In whispers of dawn, we lay our claim,
To a world alive, never the same.

Subtle Transformations

Colors shift as seasons change,
In subtle ways, life feels so strange.
Leaves flutter down, a gentle sigh,
In every ending, new dreams lie.

Breezes carry tales of old,
In every whisper, memories unfold.
Together we wander through the scenes,
Transformations weave through our dreams.

Each moment crafted, pure and real,
In this together, we learn to feel.
From dusk till dawn, a story spins,
In subtle transformations, love begins.

As sunlight fades, stars come alive,
In these changes, our spirits thrive.
With every heartbeat, every sigh,
In this festive time, we learn to fly.

The Awakening of Colors

In the garden, hues collide,
Petals whisper, colors guide,
Sunlight dances on the leaves,
Nature wakes, the heart believes.

Joyful laughter fills the air,
Butterflies float without a care,
Every shade a sweet surprise,
Life unfolds before our eyes.

Crimson reds and golden yellows,
Sparkling greens, the touch of fellows,
A canvas brushed by gentle hands,
The world awakes, our spirit stands.

Harmonies of life resound,
In every corner, beauty found,
A festive cheer, a vibrant scene,
In colors bright, we dance and dream.

The Symphony of Daybreak

Morning light breaks through the night,
Birds awaken with pure delight,
Strings of laughter fill the sky,
A symphony as dreams fly high.

Golden rays on dewdrops gleam,
Nature's chorus flows like a stream,
Every note a joyful sound,
In this moment, love is found.

Festive whispers through the trees,
Gentle breezes stir with ease,
Colors blend in sweet embrace,
A melody that time can't chase.

As shadows lift, our hearts ignite,
In the rhythm of the light,
With every pulse, the world awakes,
A joyous dance, for love's sweet sake.

Wings of the Celestial Rise

Underneath the vast expanse,
Feathers glide and spirits dance,
Celestial bodies light the way,
In festive spirit, we will sway.

With each dawn, our dreams take flight,
Wings unfurl in morning light,
A symphony of hopes anew,
In vibrant hues, our hearts break through.

Above the clouds, we find our grace,
In unity, we share this space,
The sky adorned with radiant beams,
Together we weave our dreams.

Onward to the skies we soar,
The universe, our great encore,
With laughter, love, and purest sighs,
We embrace the wings of the skies.

Dance of the Elusive Dawn

In twilight's hush, a dance begins,
With whispers soft, the night rescinds,
Moonlight fades, a new day calls,
In joyous rhythm, the darkness falls.

Colors swirl in morning's grace,
A waltz of light, a sweet embrace,
Shadows cast and spirits rise,
In this dance, the heart complies.

Every step a vibrant flair,
Nature joins the grand affair,
From the earth to skies above,
In the dance, we find our love.

Elusive dawn, a fleeting kiss,
In unity, we find our bliss,
With every twirl, the world will see,
The magic of our harmony.

Voyage of the Sun's Kiss

The sun climbs high, a golden sphere,
Its warmth spreads wide, the skies are clear.
Children laugh, their spirits arise,
A tapestry woven beneath bright skies.

Picnics spread on the verdant green,
Joyful faces, a vibrant scene.
Laughter echoed, sweet melodies sung,
A world alive, with hearts that are young.

Kites take flight, on breezy trails,
Weaving dreams as daylight prevails.
Colors collide in a jubilant swirl,
A celebration of life, as moments unfurl.

As twilight descends, the stars ignite,
The dance of dusk, a dazzling sight.
We gather close, our spirits entwined,
In the voyage of love, where hearts are aligned.

Ethereal Horizon

A canvas vast, where colors blend,
The sky's embrace, a joyous trend.
Waves of cerulean kiss the shore,
With whispers of echoes that ever implore.

Birds take wing, in graceful flight,
Painting tales in the morning light.
Each brush of wind, a harmonious tune,
As dreams awaken beneath the moon.

In the garden bright, petals sway,
With laughter blooming, a grand display.
Butterflies dance, in waltzes of glee,
The ethereal horizon, wild and free.

As night draws near, lanterns glow,
A symphony of light, a vibrant show.
We gather 'round, under the stars' kiss,
Celebrating life, in magical bliss.

Dancing Colors of Dawn

A flicker of light, breaks the night,
As dawn spills gold, a wondrous sight.
The horizon blushes, in vibrant hues,
Awakening dreams, where hope renews.

Chirping birds, a melodic cheer,
Echoes of joy, that all can hear.
Children run, with hearts that soar,
Welcoming warmth, forevermore.

Glimmers of dew, on emerald grass,
Moments of magic, as hours pass.
Colors collide, in the morning breeze,
A dance of life, that aims to please.

As day unfolds, with laughter and song,
Together we revel, where we belong.
In the colors of dawn, our spirits ignited,
In this festivity, our hearts delighted.

Celestial Feathers in Flight

Upon the breeze, feathers sway high,
A ballet of beauty, that fills the sky.
Whispers of wonder, in gentle arcs,
As dreams take flight, igniting sparks.

Glistening wings, in sunlight's embrace,
Chasing the clouds, in a joyful race.
Colors unfurl, in splendor divine,
A tapestry woven, where spirits align.

In the vale of laughter, we twirl and spin,
Playing beneath the bright, cheerful din.
Celestial dances, in radiant light,
Where hearts unite, with pure delight.

As evening descends, and stars appear,
We gather close, in love sincere.
Celestial feathers, in night's soft glow,
A celebration of life, forever to flow.

Flights of Morning Reverie

Beneath the sky, a canvas bright,
Colors dance in morning light.
Joyful hearts with laughter ring,
As nature wakes, our spirits sing.

With every breeze, a whisper flows,
In golden rays, the magic grows.
Each flower blooms, a burst of cheer,
Embracing life, the day draws near.

Clouds like cotton, soft and white,
Drift along, a wondrous sight.
Birds take flight, their song divine,
Inviting all to share the shine.

As sun ascends, the world ignites,
With hope anew, the soul delights.
In morning's glow, dreams take their flight,
In this reverie, all feels right.

The Luminescent Path

Through forests deep, where shadows play,
A luminescent path leads the way.
Twinkling lights like stars on ground,
In this magic, joy is found.

Steps of wonder, softly tread,
Enchanting dreams in petals spread.
The air alive with festive cheer,
Guiding all who dare draw near.

Night blooms bright with vibrant hues,
A melody sung in whispered views.
Each turn reveals a secret place,
Where time stands still, a warm embrace.

With every heartbeat, the joy expands,
In this realm of dreams, life commands.
Together we stroll, with smiles aglow,
On this luminescent path, we flow.

Parables of Dawning Light

In whispers soft, the night departs,
Dawn weaves tales in glowing arts.
With every hue, a story shared,
Of moments lived and hearts laid bare.

Golden rays kiss the earth anew,
Waking dreams, our hopes pursue.
Fragments of joy in bright array,
Celebrate the coming day.

As shadows wane, our spirits rise,
In laughter's glow, the past denies.
In unity, we'll share the lore,
Of dawning light and hearts that soar.

Each story told, a spark ignites,
In festive cheer, we claim our rights.
Together we dance, in pure delight,
Embracing life in dawning light.

Glide of the Illuminated Seraph

In twilight's glow, the seraphs glide,
With wings of gold, they float beside.
A gentle breeze, their whispers clear,
In every heart, they sow good cheer.

They twirl and spin, through dreams they soar,
With laughter bright, they softly implore:
To share our joys and let them rise,
In every soul, a light that ties.

Beneath the stars, they paint the sky,
A canvas vast, where hopes can fly.
With festive grace, they light the way,
Guiding all through night to day.

So let us join, this dance divine,
With illuminated seraphs, intertwined.
In this embrace, we'll find delight,
As we celebrate this wondrous night.

Murmurs of Celestial Illumination

Whispers dancing on the breeze,
Stars reflecting in our eyes,
Fireflies weave a gentle tease,
While laughter echoes through the skies.

Joyful hearts in vibrant sway,
Colors sparkling, bold and bright,
As night turns into gleeful day,
In the embrace of pure delight.

Let us gather, hands entwined,
Underneath this canopy,
Unspoken bonds forever bind,
As time unfolds in harmony.

So raise a glass, let spirits soar,
To every moment we adore,
In the dance of night, we're free,
Murmurs hum our jubilee.

Textures of the Rising Light

Morning kisses with soft grace,
Golden hues stretch far and wide,
Nature wears her bright embrace,
As shadows fleetingly subside.

Sweet aromas fill the air,
Baking bread, fresh and divine,
Laughter shared, we have such flair,
In the warmth, our spirits shine.

With every color, life awakes,
Canvas painted, pure delight,
Pledges made and memories take,
Rooted firm in morning light.

Let's weave stories, rich and grand,
In this tapestry we find,
Together, here, hand in hand,
Unity in heart and mind.

Vistas of the Vibrant Dawn

Emerging rays of sunshine greet,
Meadows dressed in jeweled dew,
Birds on high, their songs repeat,
In this dawn, the world feels new.

Faces bright with hopeful dreams,
The sky reveals a brilliant hue,
Nature's morn, with playful gleams,
Whispers of a love so true.

In the rustle of the trees,
Every branch a tale to tell,
Fill your heart with melodies,
As time casts its enchanting spell.

Celebrate the days to come,
With every breath, the world will bloom,
In vibrant threads of joy succumb,
Together we shall chase the gloom.

Cradles of Celestial Glow

Night unfolds with a velvet touch,
Moonlight dances on the sea,
Stars like diamonds shine so much,
In their glow, we feel so free.

Voices hum a soothing tune,
Dreamers weave the tales of old,
Underneath the silver moon,
Mysteries and stories told.

Hearts encircled in embrace,
Warmth ignites the chilly air,
Joyful laughter finds its place,
In the circle we all share.

As the night whispers goodnight,
With every glow, our dreams take flight,
Cradled in this cosmic show,
Eternal bonds in love shall grow.

The Lettered Skies of Dawn

As daylight spills on canvas wide,
The colors dance, a joyful ride.
Each hue a letter, bright and bold,
Tales of warmth and dreams retold.

The sun awakes with golden cheer,
Whispers of hope for all to hear.
Birds take flight in vibrant arcs,
Joining nature's festive marks.

Clouds wear crowns of softest hue,
In splendid skies, a joy anew.
Laughter rings where shadows fade,
In the dawn, our fears invade.

Gathered hearts, we share this scene,
In every corner, joy is seen.
The lettered skies, our spirits lift,
A treasured, timeless, glowing gift.

Brushes of Celestial Joy

With brushes dipped in starlight's gleam,
We paint our dreams, ignite the beam.
Colors pour like laughter's tune,
In cosmic realms, beneath the moon.

Galaxies spin in gentle sway,
Unfolding hopes in bright display.
Each stroke creates a world of bliss,
A canvas forged from friendship's kiss.

Brushes twirl, releasing cheer,
As joy cascades, we hold it dear.
With every color, a story unfolds,
In jubilant whispers, the universe holds.

So let us dance 'neath twinkling lights,
In this gala of endless nights.
With brushes poised, our hearts ignite,
Creating sparks in shared delight.

Luminescent Journeys Await

Bright horizons call us near,
As friendships bloom, we share a cheer.
With every step, new paths unfold,
In stories told, our hearts consoled.

Adventure sings in every breeze,
In laughter's wake, our spirits seize.
Shimmering dreams like stars ignite,
Guiding us through the joyful night.

Luminescent trails we tread,
With courage lighting where we're led.
Each moment shared a precious thread,
In this tapestry of joy we spread.

Together we chase the dawn's embrace,
In every challenge, we find our place.
With open hearts, the journey's bright,
A festive embrace, our spirits' flight.

Echoes of the Morning Song

Awake, the world begins to sing,
In harmony, the day takes wing.
Nature's chorus, bright and clear,
Welcomes each heart, drawing near.

Echoes spill like morning light,
Illuminating dreams so bright.
With every note, the joy appears,
In laughter shared, we cast our fears.

Birds weave tales in rhythmic flight,
Their melodies bring pure delight.
Harmonies of hope arise,
Filling us with sweet surprise.

So join the song, let spirits soar,
In celebration, forever more.
Echoes linger, a tune divine,
In every moment, love enshrined.

The Dawn's Embrace

Golden rays break through the night,
Whispers of the day take flight.
Laughter rings in the soft light,
Hearts awaken, pure delight.

Colors dance in skies so bright,
Joyful spirits, burning bright.
Hand in hand, we feel the cheer,
In this moment, love is near.

Blooming flowers in the dew,
Nature's canvas, fresh and new.
Every breath, a sweet embrace,
Together, we find our place.

The world unfolds, a festive show,
Hope and warmth in endless flow.
Celebrate the day's first glance,
In the dawn, we all shall dance.

Feathers of the Eastern Horizon

Balloons rise into the sky,
With every laugh, our spirits fly.
Glimmers bright, like dreams unveiled,
In the breeze, our joy exhaled.

Kites adorned with vibrant flair,
Flapping gently in the air.
Children's cheers and playful shouts,
In this wonder, joy abounds.

Dancing shadows paint the ground,
Echoes of delight resound.
Feathers float on whispers free,
In this fest, we dare to be.

Eyes alight with hope and dreams,
Life is bursting at the seams.
With each breath, we lift and soar,
On this horizon, we want more.

Kites of the Morning Glow

Morning gleams with colors bright,
Kites soaring, a wondrous sight.
Breezes play with gleeful sounds,
Celebrations all around.

Joyful voices fill the air,
Magic woven everywhere.
Wisps of yellow, pink, and blue,
Carried on the winds so true.

Every heart is light and free,
Chasing dreams with glee and glee.
Waving hands in the sunlight,
Together, all feels just right.

In the sky, our hopes ascend,
Creating stories without end.
Kites of joy and love we send,
In this day, our hearts transcend.

Threads of the Radiant Day

Threads of gold through fields they weave,
In this moment, we believe.
Laughter echoes, sweet and clear,
Uniting all, both far and near.

Singing songs of joy and cheer,
Radiant smiles chase off fear.
Hand in hand, we spin and twirl,
In this dance, our hearts unfurl.

Joyful feasts laid out with care,
Desserts and treats, a feast to share.
Together, side by side we stand,
Crafting memories, hand in hand.

Threads of love, a tapestry,
Woven in our revelry.
As the sun dips down to rest,
We hold each moment, feeling blessed.

Hues of the Morning Whispers

Soft pastels awaken the sky,
Laughter dances on morning's sigh.
Golden rays skip on dew-kissed blades,
Nature hums as daylight parades.

Birds unfold their vibrant wings,
Chirping notes as the day sings.
Joy threads through each leafy limb,
As the world's colors begin to brim.

A canvas painted in joy's embrace,
Sunrise sprinkles warmth and grace.
Whispers of life, fresh and bright,
Wrap the heart in pure delight.

Glorious hues in a joyful flight,
Overflowing with hope, pure and light.
Morning whispers, a festival grand,
In every corner of this blessed land.

Celestial Dance of Day's First Light

The sky awakes to a dance divine,
Twinkling stars in the sunlight shine.
Morning spreads her golden arms,
Embracing all with loving charms.

Sunrise twirls on the horizon wide,
Throwing shadows away, they glide.
Joyful breezes kiss each face,
While flowers bloom in bright embrace.

Children laugh in the morning glow,
Chasing shadows wherever they go.
Nature plays its harmonious tune,
As the sun ignites the afternoon.

Awash with colors, life unfolds,
In every heart, a story told.
The celestial dance brings us near,
In this festive moment, devoid of fear.

Ethereal Skylings Unfolding

Winds whisper stories of skies so blue,
Cotton clouds drift, soft and true.
Gentle rays paint the dawn with cheer,
Each moment savored, each laugh, sincere.

Fields glimmer like a sea of gold,
Nature unfolds, a sight to behold.
In every petal, a secret shared,
In the sun's embrace, all hearts are bared.

Skylings gather in their festive play,
Brightening dreams as they dance and sway.
Joyful echoes resonate and abide,
In this magical world, we take pride.

With every heartbeat, the day expands,
In unity, life forever stands.
Ethereal skylings in vibrant flight,
Crafting a symphony of pure delight.

Tales of the Radiant Horizon

The horizon glows with tales untold,
A canvas of wonder, rich and bold.
Colors collide in a festive array,
As night whispers gently goodbye to day.

Glimmers of hope in the evening light,
Filling our hearts with a sheer delight.
Stories woven in shades of warm hues,
Reviving our spirits as daylight renews.

In the dance of dusk, shadows play,
Carrying dreams as they drift away.
Laughter lingers on every breeze,
Echoes of joy among the trees.

Each twilight spark with a vibrant cheer,
Unveiling moments we hold so dear.
As tales of life in colors ignite,
We celebrate this wondrous night.

Ethereal Ascent

In the sky where dreams take flight,
Stars do dance, a cheerful sight.
Whispers of joy, soft and sweet,
Gathered hearts in rhythm beat.

Golden hues paint the air,
Laughter flows without a care.
Joyful echoes all around,
In this bliss, true love is found.

Clouds like cotton, soft and bright,
Lift us high, into the light.
With every smile, spirits soar,
Ethereal, we crave for more.

Together we chase the dawn,
In this realm, we feel reborn.
Magic swirls in every glance,
Life transforms into a dance.

Wings of Dawn

As the sun breaks through the haze,
Morning light begins to blaze.
Birds take flight with joyous song,
Nature's choir, free and strong.

Petals open, colors bloom,
Filling hearts with sweet perfume.
With each ray, hope starts to rise,
Painting smiles across the skies.

Winds of change begin to play,
Bringing warmth to greet the day.
Hands united, hearts as one,
Joyful laughter has begun.

In the glow of vibrant morn,
We embrace what's yet unborn.
With wings of dawn, we take flight,
Chasing dreams in morning light.

A Symphony of Colors

Brushstrokes of joy paint the scene,
Every hue begins to gleam.
Dancing in the vibrant air,
Life's a canvas, bright and rare.

Laughter twirls like autumn leaves,
Magic happens, heart believes.
Every note a cherished sound,
A symphony of love profound.

Feel the pulse of joyous thrill,
As the world, our hearts, it fills.
Harmony in every glance,
Inviting all to join the dance.

With arms open, we embrace,
Every moment, every place.
In this tapestry of cheer,
Colors weave our stories here.

Luminous Journey

Step by step, we light the way,
Path aglow, bright as day.
Stars above in twinkling cheer,
Guide our hearts, keep dreams near.

With every turn, surprises bloom,
Joy ignites, dispels the gloom.
Hand in hand, with eyes aglow,
Together we create the flow.

In this journey, souls unite,
Casting shadows into light.
Chasing wonders, side by side,
On this wave, we take the ride.

Through the night, we pave the path,
Sharing laughter, love, and laughs.
In our hearts, the spark will grow,
Luminous, the dreams will flow.

Dawn's Embrace

In the morn, a soft glow,
Whispers of joy begin to flow.
Colors dance in warm embrace,
Nature's smile, a gentle grace.

Laughter fills the vibrant air,
Joyous hearts, without a care.
Buds bloom forth, in bright array,
A celebration of the day.

Sunbeams play on pools of dew,
Each ray a promise, fresh, anew.
With every breeze, a cheerful song,
Together we all belong.

As shadows fade, we raise a cheer,
For cherished moments we hold dear.
In this dawn, let spirits rise,
Festive love beneath the skies.

Celestial Feathers

Stars twinkle in the velvet night,
A cosmic dance, pure delight.
Whispers of dreams on night's soft breath,
Woven with laughter that knows no death.

With moonlight draping all around,
Magic of the universe found.
Feathers of light in every heart,
In this moment, we're never apart.

Fireflies flicker in joyful flight,
Guiding us through the tranquil night.
Voices raised in songs of glee,
Together in this harmony.

Celestial wonders in our view,
Underneath a sky so blue.
In the cosmos, our spirits soar,
A festive night, forevermore.

Radiant Skies

Sunrise paints the heavens bright,
Golden hues burst forth with light.
A tapestry of vibrant colors,
Together we dance with joyous shudders.

Clouds adorned in pastel shades,
Nature's palette, no charades.
With laughter ringing through the air,
We gather here, beyond compare.

Kites flying high in gentle breeze,
Children laughing, purest of ease.
Every heart beats in time's sweet song,
Celebrating where we all belong.

As evening falls, the stars ignite,
A symphony of silver light.
We raise our eyes to skies so grand,
In this moment, hand in hand.

Chasing the Light

Through fields of gold, we run and play,
Chasing the light of a brand new day.
With every step, our spirits soar,
Adventures wait, we ask for more.

The sun's warm kiss upon our skin,
A joyful dance, let the day begin.
Friendship blooms in laughter's sound,
In this joyous world, we're homeward bound.

Picnics spread on soft green grass,
Moments treasured, fleeting yet vast.
Stories shared as stars appear,
Capturing memories we hold dear.

As twilight whispers its sweet refrain,
We gather 'round, sunshine in our veins.
Chasing the light, we celebrate,
In this vibrant life, our hearts elate.

The Palette of New Horizons

Colors bloom in every glance,
Joyful hearts in vibrant dance.
With laughter painted in the air,
We craft our dreams, a life to share.

Balloons rise like whispers bright,
Cascading hope in morning light.
Every cheer a brushstroke bold,
As stories of joy begin to unfold.

Hands entwined, we take the stage,
A canvas bright, we turn the page.
With every heartbeat, colors sing,
In festive spirits, blessings bring.

Together we weave a tapestry,
Of love and joy, in harmony.
The palette swirls with endless grace,
In new horizons, we find our place.

Chronicles of the Morning Light

Awake! The dawn is casting spells,
A symphony of ringing bells.
Golden rays through windows shine,
Inviting warmth, hearts intertwine.

Soft whispers greet the world anew,
With fluttering leaves in vibrant hue.
Laughter dances on the breeze,
As life unfolds amidst the trees.

Fleeting moments, treasured sights,
A canvas filled with pure delights.
Together we embrace the morn,
In festive tales, our souls are worn.

Through the stories that we share,
Embracing joy, beyond compare.
Chronicles told in every heart,
In morning light, we find our art.

Ascendancy of the Dawn

As the sun peeks over hills,
A world awakens, joy instills.
Serene whispers fill the air,
In every step, a vibrant flair.

Colors spill through golden skies,
Inspiring hope as daylight flies.
A chorus rises, spirits free,
In every heart, a rhapsody.

Festive patterns weave and twirl,
As laughter dances, hearts unfurl.
With every moment, shining bright,
We celebrate the dawning light.

Together, hand in hand we stride,
On waves of joy, together ride.
The day awaits, a grand adventure,
In the dawn's embrace, we find our treasure.

Tidal Echoes of Morning Voyage

Gentle tides caress the shore,
With every wave, we long for more.
Sunrise glimmers on the sea,
A canvas where our spirits flee.

The horizon calls, a distant song,
In this voyage, we belong.
Salty air and breezy cheer,
Every heartbeat drawing near.

Echoes of laughter fill the air,
As joy emerges everywhere.
In pockets rich with life's embrace,
We weave our dreams in time and space.

Together sailing towards the light,
In morning's glow, the future bright.
With tidal waves and hopes unfurled,
We journey forth, our dreams unfurled.

The Glow of New Beginnings

In the dawn's embrace we cheer,
Laughter dances, joy draws near.
Colors bloom in vibrant light,
Hope awakens, hearts take flight.

Balloons rising in the air,
Whispers sweet, a gentle prayer.
Together we will laugh and play,
In this glow of bright new day.

Cakes adorned with sparkles bright,
Welcoming the day with delight.
Every moment, love unfurls,
As we celebrate our worlds.

With open arms, we gather round,
In the magic, love is found.
New beginnings, vibrant, true,
A festive spirit shared by you.

Paintbrush of the Twilight Sky

The sky is painted shades of gold,
As stories of the night unfold.
With stars that wink and softly gleam,
Nature's canvas, a waking dream.

Lanterns float like whispers sweet,
As laughter echoes down the street.
Colors blend in twilight's grace,
Creating wonders we embrace.

Drums are beating, spirits soar,
Echoes of joy we can't ignore.
In the hues of dusk's caress,
We find our hearts in happiness.

With every brush, the night ignites,
As magic glows in soft moonlights.
Together, under starlit sky,
We dance and twirl, our spirits high.

Flight Beyond the Morning Veil

With wings of hope, we rise anew,
Through misty dreams, the sun breaks through.
A gentle breeze, the world awakes,
At dawn's soft touch, the silence shakes.

Colors burst, the sky ignites,
As laughter fills the gentle heights.
Every heartbeat, a vibrant song,
In this moment, we all belong.

Chasing shadows, bright and free,
Flying high, just you and me.
The morning sparkles, fresh and bright,
In joyful flight, we chase the light.

With every breath, we feel the thrill,
As dreams take shape, and hearts do fill.
Beyond the veil, our spirits gleam,
In this embrace, we live the dream.

Ethereal Light in Motion

In fields of gold, we twirl and spin,
As sunlight dances on our skin.
With laughter flowing all around,
In every corner, joy is found.

A flash of color, vibrant hues,
In celebrations, we can choose.
To lift our voices, share our dreams,
In this moment, life redeems.

Through every step, the world ignites,
In a tapestry of festive lights.
All together, hearts align,
In the rhythm, our joy will shine.

Ethereal wonders in the air,
A dance of spirits, beyond compare.
Hand in hand, we find our way,
In this magic, forever stay.

Feathered Dreams

In the sky, the birds take flight,
Colors dance in pure delight.
Whispers of joy fill the air,
As laughter twirls without a care.

Banners flutter in the breeze,
Underneath the blooming trees.
Children play with smiles so wide,
In this moment, hearts abide.

Songs of friendship, sweet and clear,
Echo softly, spreading cheer.
Every moment blissful, bright,
Underneath the stars tonight.

With feathered dreams high above,
We gather round to share our love.
Let the festive spirit soar,
As we dance forevermore.

Colors of a New Day

Morning breaks with golden hues,
Painting skies with vibrant views.
Joyful hearts and hopeful eyes,
Beneath the warmth of rising skies.

Nature wakes in calm surprise,
As sunlight dances, laughter flies.
Every leaf a story tells,
In the air, a magic swells.

Cups are raised with friendly cheer,
As we gather, loved ones near.
Colors brighten every face,
In this joyful, warm embrace.

With each dawn, new hopes arise,
Shining bright, like summer skies.
In this moment, we are free,
Together, one big family.

Light's Gentle Caress

Softly glows the evening light,
Wrapping all in warmth so bright.
Candles flicker, shadows dance,
In this moment, we take a chance.

Whispers of love fill the air,
As we gather, hearts laid bare.
With every smile, a bond we weave,
In the joy that we believe.

Laughter echoes through the night,
Under stars that gleam so bright.
Clinking glasses, toasting dreams,
In life's tapestry, friendship gleams.

With light's caress, we celebrate,
Every memory we create.
In this circle, warm and true,
Together, we can start anew.

Soaring Through the Twilight

As the sun in silence dips,
Nighttime's beauty gently sips.
Mountains echo with soft songs,
To where the heart of nature belongs.

Fireflies dance in twilight's glow,
Guiding dreams where rivers flow.
In this hour, spirits rise high,
As colors blend in the evening sky.

Together we embrace the night,
Underneath the moon's soft light.
Every soul begins to sway,
In this festive, wild ballet.

With whispers shared and stories spun,
We celebrate, we laugh, we run.
Soaring through this magic tide,
In unity, we take a ride.

Gale of the Opening Sky

In the breeze, laughter spins,
Colors dance, joy begins,
Waves of light, in the air,
Hearts ignite, without a care.

Fireworks burst, a sparkling show,
Faces glow, in the night's flow,
Whispers of dreams, sweet and bright,
Together we bask in the shared light.

Music swells, an infectious beat,
Feet in rhythm, we turn and meet,
Hand in hand, we twirl and sway,
Embracing magic, come what may.

As stars twinkle, in lively cheer,
Hope and laughter, drawing near,
In this gale, spirits soar high,
A celebration beneath the sky.

Feathered Visions in Flight

Eagles soar, in golden rays,
Chasing dreams, through open ways,
Wings of hope, lifting our souls,
Whispers of freedom, making us whole.

Balloons rise, in shades so bright,
A tapestry woven, pure delight,
With every glance, horizons tease,
A dance of colors, carried by breeze.

Laughter leaps, from every voice,
Underneath the trees, we rejoice,
In this moment, the world feels right,
Feathered visions take their flight.

As day fades, a canvas wide,
In this festivity, hearts collide,
Together we dream, together we sing,
In the dawn of joy, our spirits take wing.

Push Beyond the Daybreak's Veil

Morning light spills, soft and sweet,
Awakening hope with each heartbeat,
Golden rays break through the morn,
A fresh canvas, dreams reborn.

With each step, possibilities sprout,
In every laugh, there's no doubt,
Under the sun, we light the way,
Pushing beyond what night may sway.

Blossoms unfold, in vibrant cheer,
Nature smiles, with love sincere,
We gather close, hearts intertwined,
A festive spirit, beautifully aligned.

As shadows fade, and spirits rise,
We celebrate under painted skies,
In this moment, love prevails,
Pushing past the daybreak's veils.

The Arc of New Beginnings

A rainbow arcs o'er open fields,
Promise shines, as nature yields,
In every bloom, hope finds its place,
A festive scene, wrapped in grace.

Dancing leaves, in golden hues,
Whispers of joy, in morning's muse,
Harvesting laughter, sharing our dreams,
In this new dawn, everything gleams.

With friends beside, we raise a cheer,
Celebrating moments, year after year,
In every heart, a tale to share,
The arc of beginnings, beyond compare.

As the sun sets, casting its glow,
We know in our hearts, love will flow,
In this festival, let spirits ring,
For every ending's just a new beginning.

Celestial Awakening

In the dawn's embrace, colors ignite,
Joyful whispers weave day from night.
Stars cascade like confetti in air,
Hearts twirl and leap, free from despair.

Banners of gold in the sunlight gleam,
Children laugh and dance, living the dream.
Blossoms unfold with a fragrant cheer,
Nature awakens, springtime is here.

The laughter of friends fills the warm glow,
As heartbeats sync with the brisk river flow.
Every moment a treasure in light,
Together we bask in the festive sight.

So let us rejoice as the day unfolds,
With stories and memories, treasures untold.
In unity, we find what it means,
To celebrate life within vibrant scenes.

Flight of the Morning Star

Glistening wings in the morning light,
Whispers of hope rise, taking flight.
The canvas above bursts in hues,
A tapestry woven with bright, vibrant views.

Flutes sing a tune, inviting us near,
Echoes of laughter, the music we hear.
Each note a spark, igniting the dawn,
As shadows recede, and doubt is withdrawn.

The skies break open; they dance in delight,
Celebrations spark in the warm, golden light.
With every heartbeat, the world comes alive,
Kindred souls gather, we sing and we thrive.

So soar with the stars, let your spirit unite,
In the festival's glow, we burn ever bright.
Each moment a blessing, together we stand,
In the flight of the morning, hand in hand.

Horizon's Gift

As the sun dips down, painting the skies,
Colors collide in a duet, they rise.
The world adorned with a festive gleam,
Embraces the beauty of a vibrant dream.

Drumbeats echo from valleys so deep,
Inviting us all from a peaceful sleep.
Voices entwined in a melody sweet,
As we gather round for a joyous feast.

The flavors of laughter, the scents of delight,
Wrap around us as stars greet the night.
Every twinkle above, a wish come to life,
We dance in the warmth, forgetting our strife.

In this moment, we relish the spark,
The magic unfolds as we ride through the dark.
With love as the lantern that guides us anew,
In horizon's embrace, we're forever true.

The Dance of Fading Night

In twilight's arms, we gather to play,
As shadows retreat, welcoming day.
The moon winks softly, a mischievous glance,
Inviting our spirits to join in the dance.

With lanterns aglow, we weave through the trees,
Our laughter like music, carried by breeze.
Each step illuminated by flickering light,
In the gentle embrace of the fading night.

Whirling with joy as the stars wink in tune,
The horizon blushes, kissed by the moon.
Together we sway, the magic is real,
In this festive gathering, souls gently heal.

As dawn breaks anew, we'll cherish this sight,
Remember the dance of the soft, fading night.
With hearts intertwined, we'll forever belong,
In the echoes of laughter, our spirits stay strong.

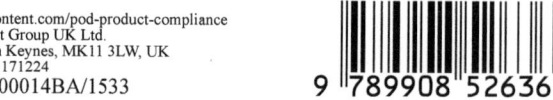

www.ingramcontent.com/pod-product-compliance
Ingram Content Group UK Ltd.
Pitfield, Milton Keynes, MK11 3LW, UK
UKHW020123171224
452675UK00014BA/1533